Sketches in Ivory
SACRED ARRANGEMENTS FOR PIANO

ISBN 978-1-4768-7716-7

Shawnee Press

EXCLUSIVELY DISTRIBUTED BY

7777 W. BLUEMOUND RD. P.O. BOX 13819 MILWAUKEE, WI 53213

Visit Shawnee Press Online at
www.shawneepress.com

Visit Hal Leonard Online at
www.halleonard.com

FOREWORD

I've always cherished the older hymns of the faith, particularly those that stem from the music of early America. I was surrounded by these hymns as a youth, and in a very real sense, the sturdy, heartfelt melodies of early American hymnody formed the soundtrack of my childhood. Needless to say, when I was given the opportunity to write a collection of piano arrangements featuring some of these old hymns, folksongs, and spirituals for Shawnee Press, I said, "Yes!" immediately!

Pianists will find a wide range of stylistic variety in this volume, and all of the selections are suitable for both worship services and recitals. It is my hope that as you prepare and perform these arrangements, these timeless melodies will come alive once again and minister to you and your listeners.

This is my first published collection of piano music and I simply could not have completed the task without the help of several wonderful people. I would like to thank Joseph Martin, Mark Hayes, Geoffrey Haydon, and Tony Harris for the countless ways they have encouraged and inspired me. Most importantly, I would like to thank Pattie, Kylie, and Sarah, my beautiful wife and children. They patiently and lovingly endure countless hours of me sitting at the piano, writing note after note...

Enjoy the music!
In Christ,

Brad

ABOUT BRAD NIX

Brad Nix currently serves as Music Department Chair and Associate Professor of Piano at Sterling College, located in Sterling, KS. His responsibilities include overseeing the department, teaching applied and group piano, music theory, aural skills, and arranging. He has also taught music appreciation, music history, piano literature, and piano pedagogy.

Brad received the Doctor of Musical Arts degree in Piano Performance from the University of Colorado at Boulder. His primary teachers include David Watkins, Geoffrey Haydon, and Andrew Cooperstock. Brad remains an active recitalist, pedagogue, and freelance pianist. He also makes frequent appearances as an adjudicator for local and statewide piano competitions.

As a composer and arranger, Brad has written for several major publishing companies and has dozens of pieces in print. In addition, several of his pieces have been awarded Editor's Choice designations. His principal composition teachers include Mark Hayes and Joseph Martin.

APPALACHIAN PRAISE

My arrangement of the hymn tune WARRENTON (from *The Sacred Harp*, 1844) is decidedly rustic and "Americana" in nature. This melody is most often paired with Robert Robinson's well-known text, "Come, Thou Fount of Every Blessing." Each verse concludes with the joyous refrain: *I am bound for the kingdom. Will you go to glory with me? Hallelujah, praise the Lord!*

LONG TIME AGO

The gorgeous melody of this early American song was a pleasure to arrange. Joseph Martin and J. Paul Williams wrote a beautiful sacred text for this secular tune in their choral anthem "Carol of Remembrance," and I had their words in mind as I crafted my arrangement: *To a tiny stable lowly, long time ago, came the Son of God most holy, long time ago.*

Words Copyright © 2000 by GlorySound and Malcolm Music (divisions of Shawnee Press, Inc.) All Rights Reserved. Used by Permission.

THERE IS A FOUNTAIN

This beautiful hymn has pointed countless people to Christ. Before my own conversion, I remember being painfully aware of the depth of my sin, and my desperate need for a Savior. The second verse always spoke to me in an intensely personal way: *The dying thief rejoiced to see that fountain in his day; and there may I, though vile as he, wash all my sins away.*

WHEN STEPHEN, FULL OF POWER AND GRACE

Stemming from the 1815 version of *Kentucky Harmony*, the hymn tune SALVATION is sometimes set to Jan Struther's text "When Stephen, Full of Power and Grace." I chose to arrange this haunting melody as a moderate jazz waltz.

LORD, I WANT TO BE A CHRISTIAN

I like to play this traditional spiritual in a fun, "stride-piano" style. This melody is usually arranged a bit more reverently than my version presented here, but I wanted to capture some of the joy and excitement that comes when a person desires a relationship with Christ, and then finds new life in Him.

INTERLUDE *(for my wife and children, Pattie, Kylie, and Sarah)*

The hymn tune MORNING SONG comes from Wyeth's *Repository of Sacred Music, Part Second*, 1813. As a child, I remember singing this melody to the stirring text "Awake, Awake to Love and Work," by G.A. Studdert-Kennedy. Originally in common time, my arrangement is set in ³/4, and features an almost relentless stream of eighth-notes, giving the music a somewhat restless quality.

COME, ALL CHRISTIANS, BE COMMITTED

The sturdy melody of BEACH SPRING (from *The Sacred Harp*, 1844) has been successfully paired with several texts throughout the years. Usually in ³/2, I chose to write my arrangement in ⁶/8 to give it a more buoyant, dance-like quality.

DEEP RIVER *(for my parents, Larry and Carol Nix)*

This heartfelt spiritual of African-American origin, features what is perhaps my favorite melody of all time. The words speak of the desire in all believers to be united with Christ and to be free from earthy toils and trials: *Deep river, my home is over Jordan. Deep river, Lord. I want to cross over into campground.*

ALL HAIL THE POWER OF JESUS' NAME

Over the years, this popular text by Edward Perronet has been set to several hymn tunes, including DIADEM and MILES LANE. I chose the tune CORONATION for my arrangement. The joyous nature of the music highlights the celebratory text: *All hail the power of Jesus' name! Let angels prostrate fall. Bring forth the royal diadem and crown Him Lord of all.*

WHEN I CAN READ MY TITLE CLEAR
(in memory of my grandmothers, Gladys Nix and Billie Cobb)

The tune PISGAH always brings to mind warm memories of my grandmothers, and, as I wrote this arrangement, my thoughts inevitably turned to them. They both loved singing the old hymns. My paternal grandmother, Gladys (affectionately known as "Ma"), was a lifetime participant in *Sacred Harp* singing sessions, and had an alto voice that many in our town said could be "heard across three counties." I'm sure both of my grandmothers are now singing the old hymns with even more joy and gusto than they ever did here on earth.

GOING HOME *(in memory of Trey and Lauren)*

This beautiful spiritual was the basis of the second movement of Antonin Dvorak's *New World Symphony*. The tender text most associated with this tune speaks of the believer's final journey home to heaven. My arrangement is dedicated to the memory of my nephew, Trey, and his beautiful wife, Lauren.

APPALACHIAN PRAISE

Tune: **WARRENTON**
Music: The Sacred Harp, 1844
Arranged by
BRAD NIX (ASCAP)

With spirit (♩ = ca. 108-112)

35028708

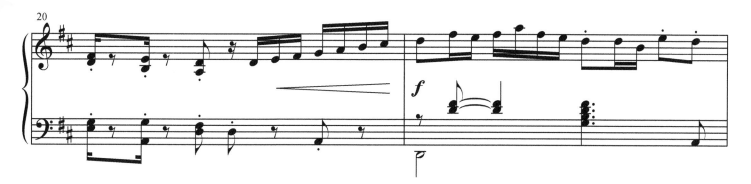

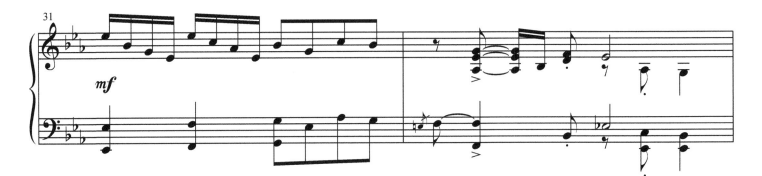

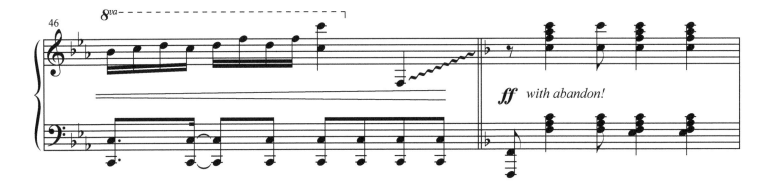

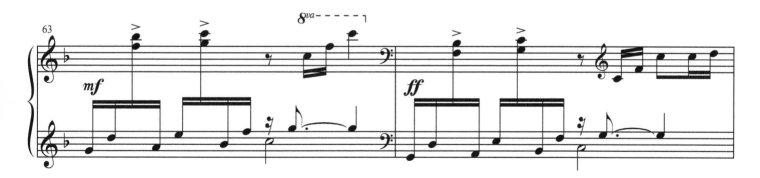

LONG TIME AGO

Tune: **LONG TIME AGO**
Music: Early American Song
Arranged by
BRAD NIX (ASCAP)

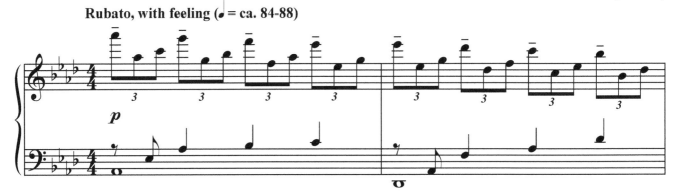

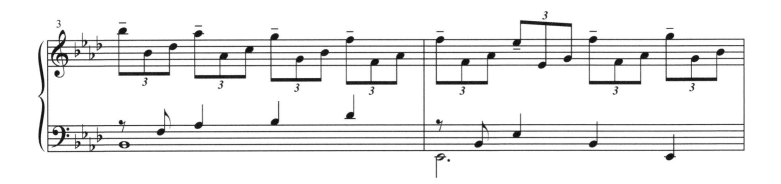

35028708

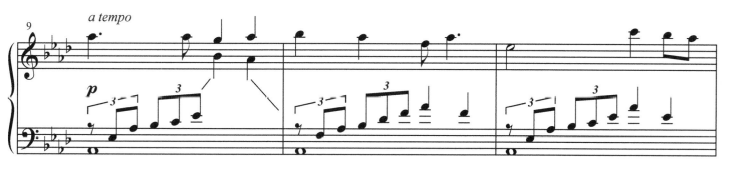

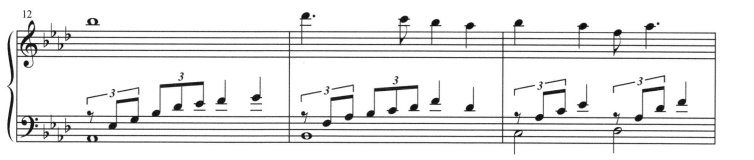

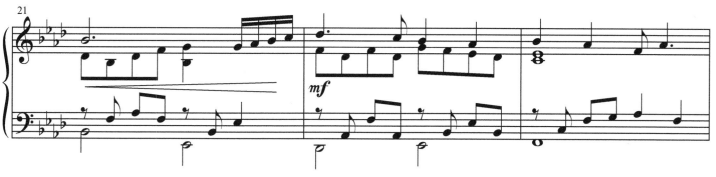

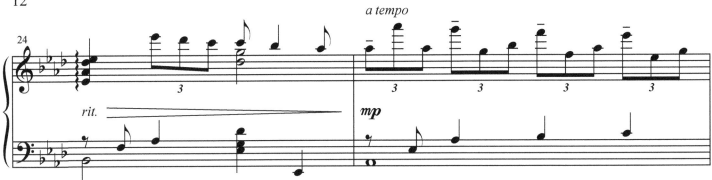

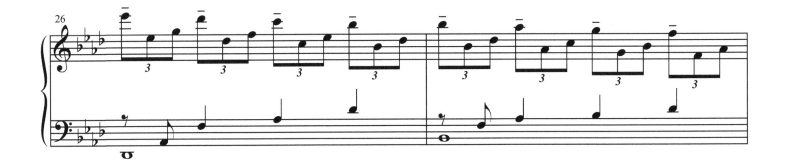

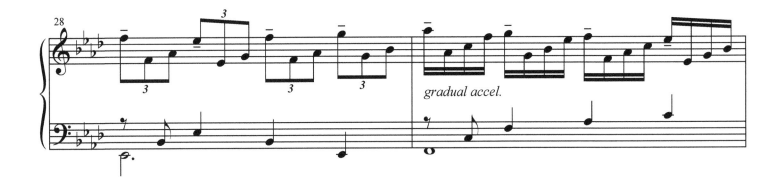

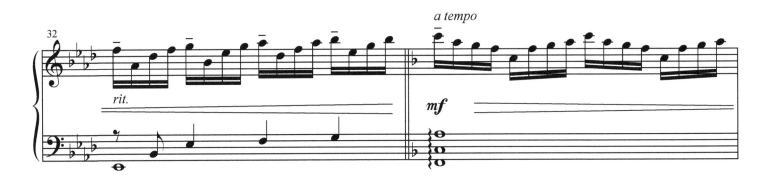

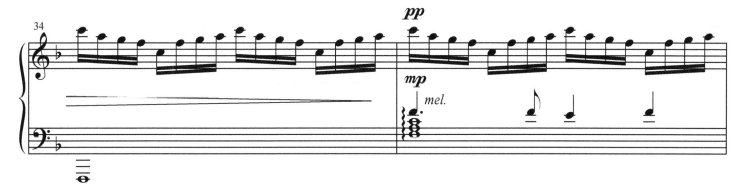

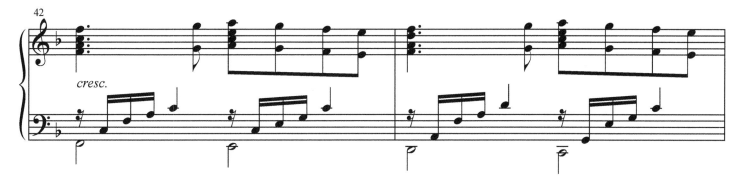

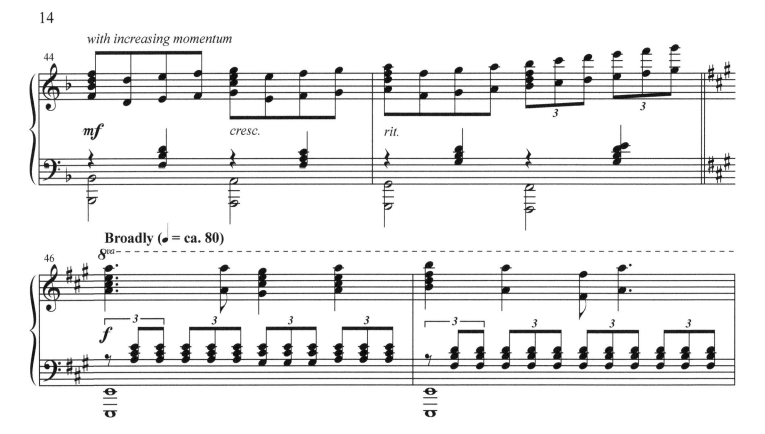

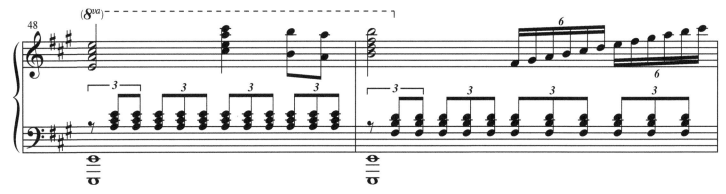

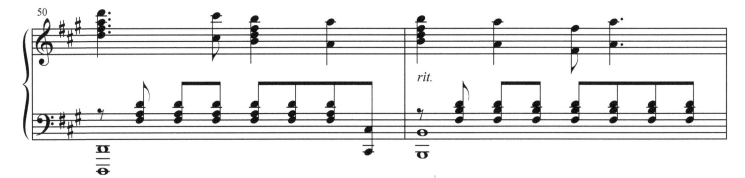

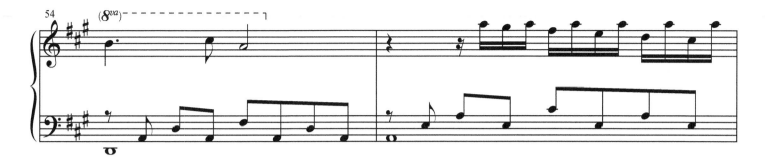

Slower, with freedom (♩ = ca. 76)

THERE IS A FOUNTAIN

Tune: **CLEANSING FOUNTAIN**
Music: Traditional American Melody
Arranged by
BRAD NIX (ASCAP)

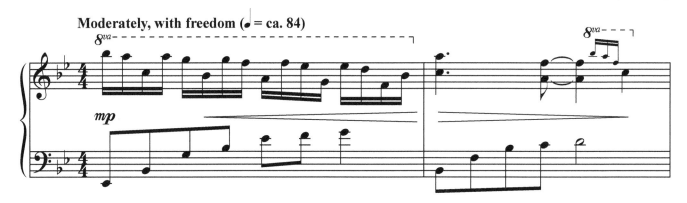

35028708

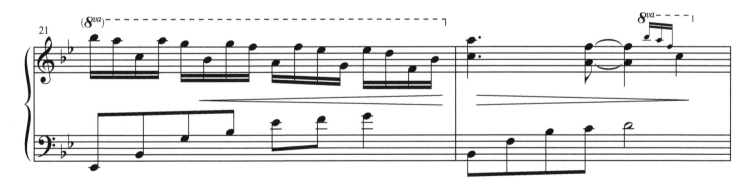

Faster, with more urgency (♩ = ca. 88)

Tempo I (♩ = ca. 84)

with momentum

a tempo

Maestoso (♩ = ca. 80)

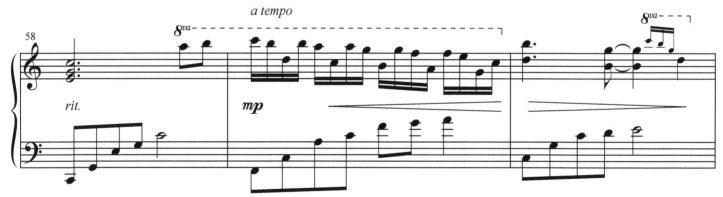

WHEN STEPHEN, FULL OF POWER AND GRACE

Tune: **SALVATION**
Music: Kentucky Harmony, 1815
Arranged by
BRAD NIX (ASCAP)

Slower (♩ = ca. 88)
even eighth notes

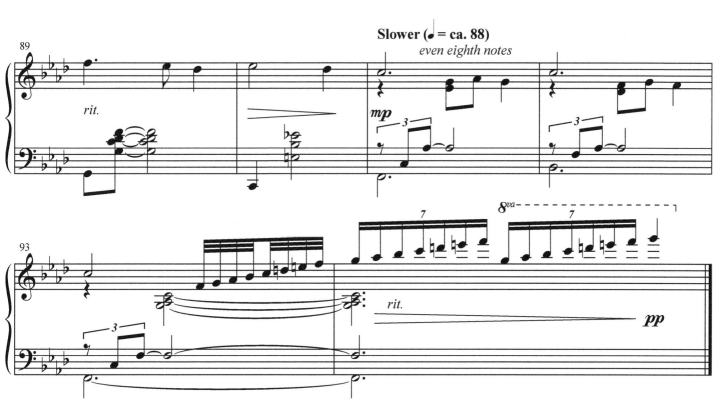

LORD, I WANT TO BE A CHRISTIAN

Tune: **I WANT TO BE A CHRISTIAN**
Music: Traditional Spiritual
Arranged by
BRAD NIX (ASCAP)

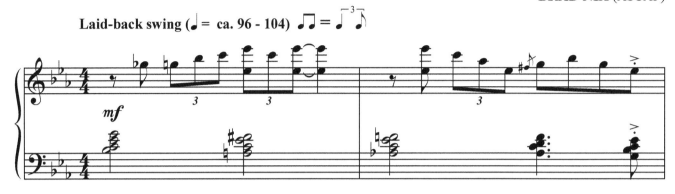

* All extended left hand chords may be rolled, or all notes except the bass notes omitted.

35028708

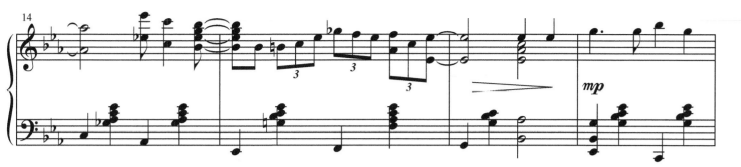

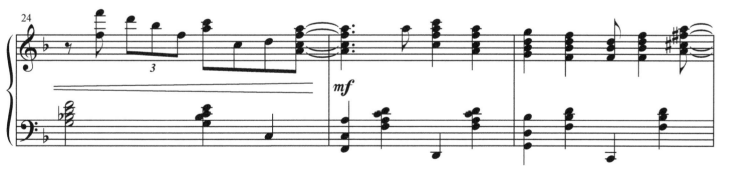

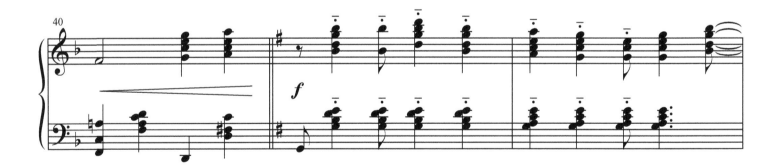

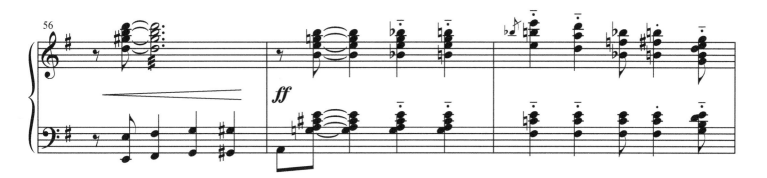

for my wife and children, Pattie, Kylie, and Sarah

INTERLUDE

Tune: **MORNING SONG**
Music: Wyeth's *Repository of Sacred Music*, 1813
Arranged by
BRAD NIX (ASCAP)

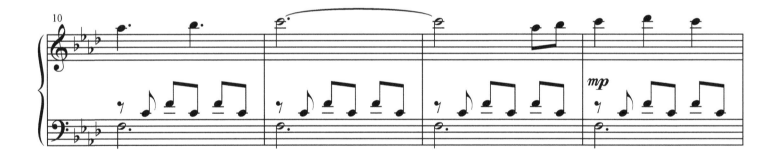

35028708

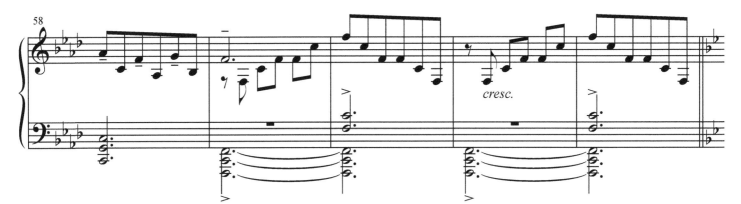

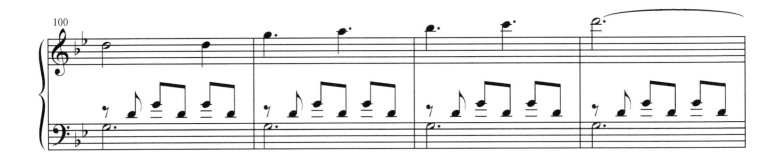

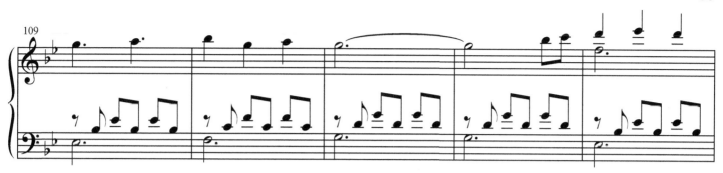

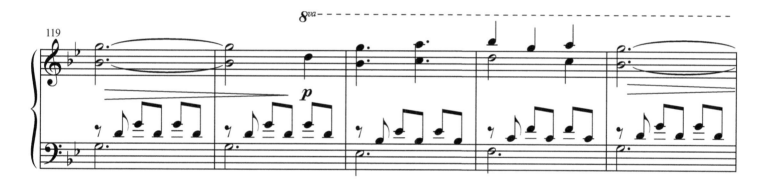

COME, ALL CHRISTIANS, BE COMMITTED

Tune: **BEACH SPRING**
Music: The Sacred Harp, 1844
Arranged by
BRAD NIX (ASCAP)

With joyful expectancy (♩. = ca. 69 or faster)

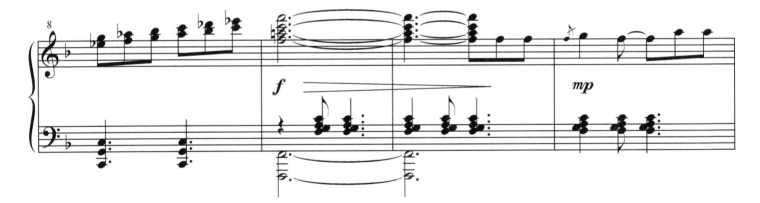

35028708

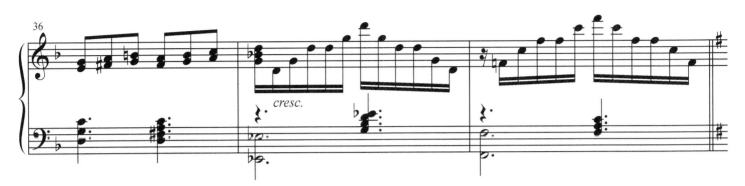

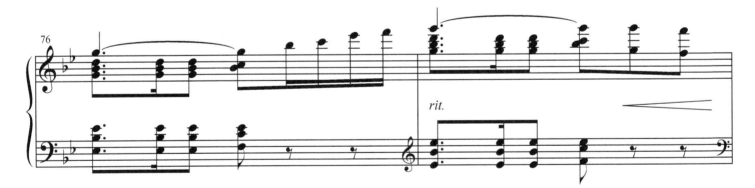

for my parents, Larry and Carol Nix

DEEP RIVER

Tune: **DEEP RIVER**
Music: Traditional Spiritual
Arranged by
BRAD NIX (ASCAP)

35028708

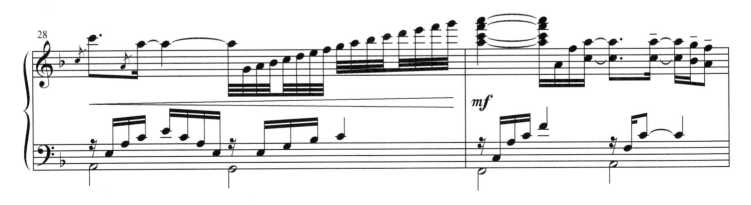

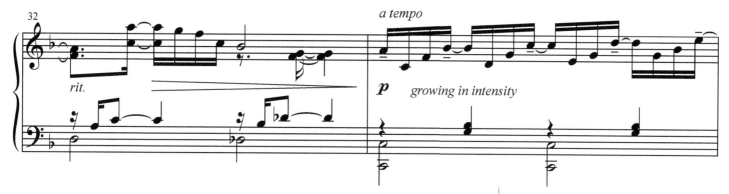

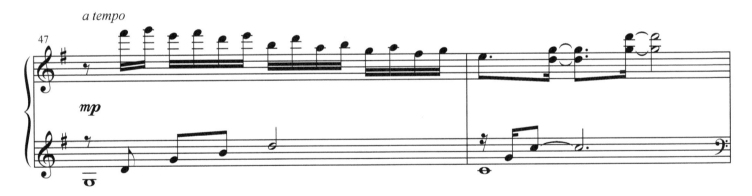

ALL HAIL THE POWER OF JESUS' NAME

Tune: **CORONATION**
Music: Oliver Holden (1765-1844)
Arranged by
BRAD NIX (ASCAP)

Bright rock feel (♩ = ca. 138)

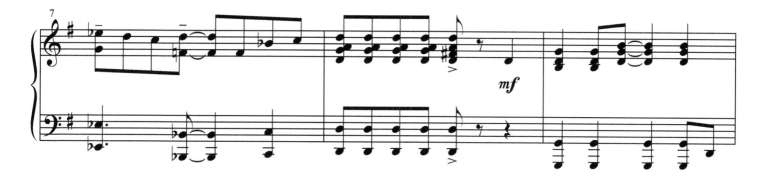

35028708

in memory of my grandmothers, Gladys Nix and Billie Cobb

WHEN I CAN READ MY TITLE CLEAR

Tune: **PISGAH**
Music: Kentucky Harmony, 1817
Arranged by
BRAD NIX (ASCAP)

Copyright © 2012 HAL LEONARD CORPORATION
International Copyright Secured. All Rights Reserved.

35028708

Maestoso (♩ = ca. 60)

Tempo I ($\sqrt{}$ = ca. 63-66)

Slower, with freedom ($\sqrt{}$ = ca. 50)

in memory of Trey and Lauren

GOING HOME

Tune: **GOIN' HOME**
Music: ANTONÍN DVOŘÁK (1841-1904)
Arranged by
BRAD NIX (ASCAP)

Slowly, with great expression (♩ = ca. 76)

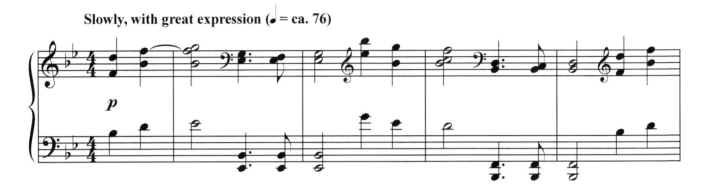

35028708

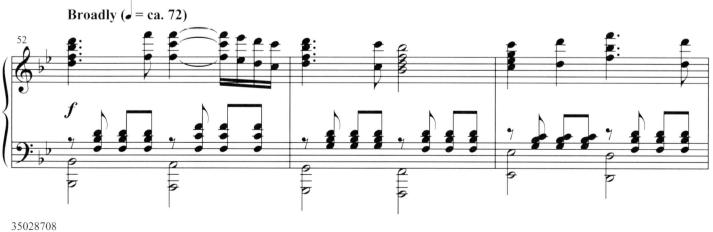